my itty-bitty bio

Gwen Frostic

Published in the United States of America by Cherry Lake Publishing
Ann Arbor, Michigan
www.cherrylakepublishing.com

Reading Adviser: Marla Conn, MS, Ed, Literacy specialist, Read-Ability, Inc.
Book Designer: Jennifer Wahl
Illustrator: Jeff Bane

Photo Credits: ©Michigan Railroad Commission/Wikimedia, 5; ©Iryna Inshyna/Shutterstock, 7; ©Bob Linearwind/Shutterstock, 9; ©Everett Collection/Shutterstock, 11; ©Virginia Jones, 13; ©Western Michigan University, 15, 19, 21, 22, 23; ©Michael Barera/Wikimedia/Creative Commons Attribution-Share Alike 4.0 International, 17; Jeff Bane, cover, 1, 6, 10, 16

Library of Congress Cataloging-in-Publication Data has been filed and is available at catalog.loc.gov

Printed in the United States of America
Corporate Graphics

table of contents

About the author: Katlin Sarantou grew up in the cornfields of Ohio. She enjoys reading and dreaming of faraway places.

About the illustrator: Jeff Bane and his two business partners own a studio along the American River in Folsom, California, home of the 1849 Gold Rush. When Jeff's not sketching or illustrating for clients, he's either swimming or kayaking in the river to relax.

my story

I was born in Michigan in 1906.

I got very sick.

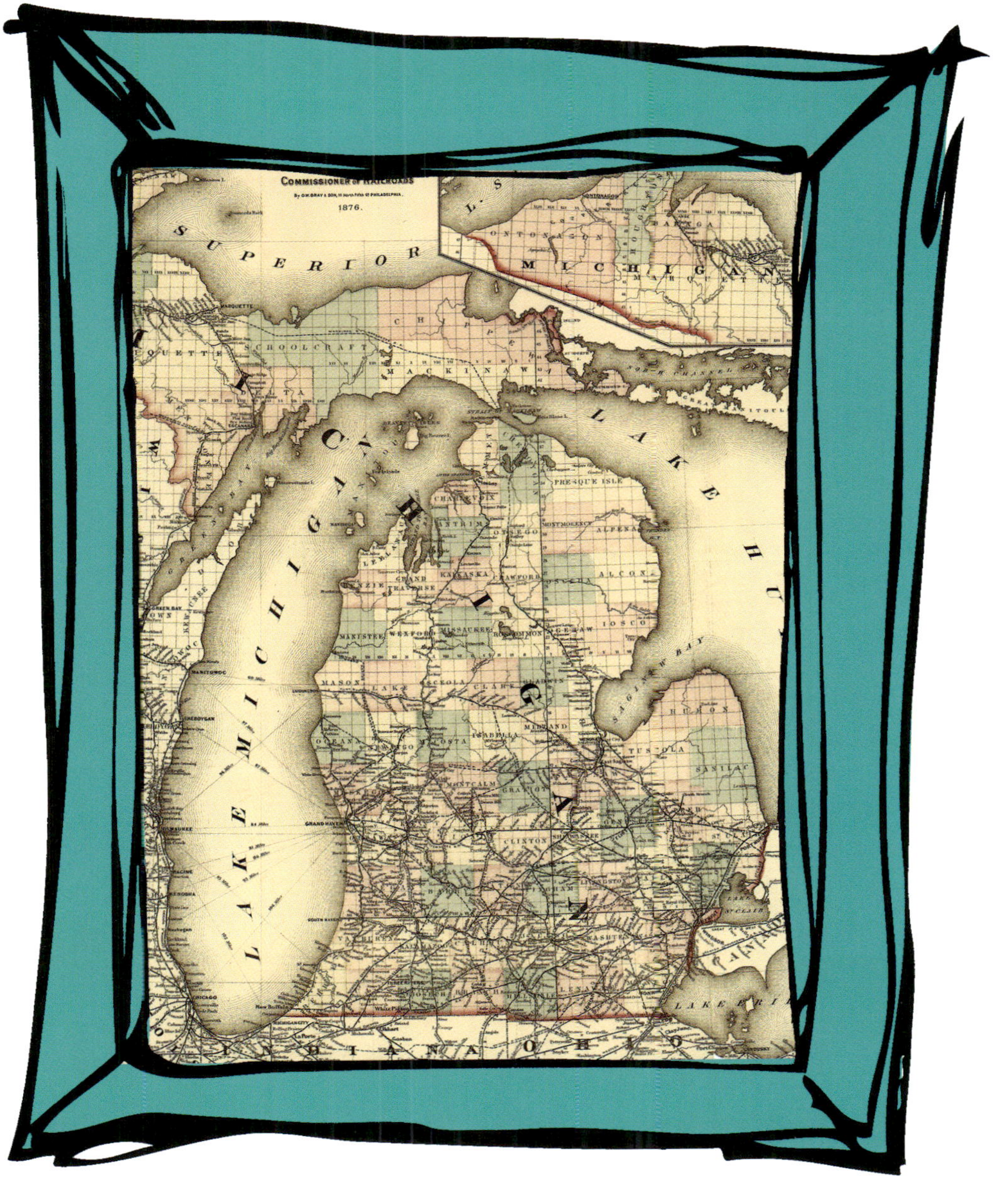
COMMISSIONER of RAILROADS
1876.
SUPERIOR
MICHIGAN
SCHOOLCRAFT
MACKINAW
LAKE HURON
LAKE MICHIGAN
MICHIGAN
PRESQUE ISLE
ALPENA
ALCONA
IOSCO
MANISTEE
WEXFORD
MASON
HURON
TUSCOLA
MIDLAND
MONTCALM
CLINTON
GRAND HAVEN
INDIANA
OHIO

My sickness made it hard to use my hands. But I didn't let it stop me. My mom **encouraged** me to draw nature.

What problem have you overcome?

I went to art school. I worked with **linoleum** blocks. I **etched** designs into them.

I made these block carvings into prints.

There was a war. I wanted to help.

I used my skills. I helped make tools to build planes.

What special skills do you have?

I wanted to sell my art.

I started a business. People didn't think a woman could do it.

I opened my shop anyway.

Gwen Frostic

I moved my shop to northern Michigan.

I designed the building myself.

My art was really popular. It still is. It reminds people that we need to protect nature.

This idea helped fuel the **environmental movement**.

What do you love about nature?

In 1986, I was **inducted** into the Michigan Women's **Hall of Fame**.

I died in 2001.

I was a successful artist. My art **inspired** people to love nature.

My shop in northern Michigan remains open today!

What would you like to ask me?

timeline

1950s

1900

Born
1906

1986

2000

Died
2001

glossary & index

glossary

encouraged (en-KUR-ijd) to help or support someone in doing something

environmental movement (en-vye-ruhn-MEN-tuhl MOOV-muhnt) people working together to protect the air, land, and water

etched (ECHD) to cut a design on a hard surface using a sharp object

hall of fame (HAWL UHV FAME) a place honoring people's accomplishments

inducted (in-DUHK-tid) admitted, to allow someone in

inspired (in-SPIRED) to feel the desire to do something

linoleum (luh-NOH-lee-uhm) a material with a strong, shiny surface, usually used to cover floors

index